THANK YOU TIMES A MILLION

MADE FOR YOU BY...

I WROTE THIS BOOK JUST FOR YOU,

_____.

BECAUSE IF THERE'S ANYONE IN THIS WHOLE CRAZY WORLD I'M SUPERBLY GRATEFUL FOR, IT'S YOU. AND I THINK YOU DESERVE TO HAVE A WHOLE BOOK DEDICATED JUST TO YOU.

I'LL ALWAYS BE
GRATEFUL FOR
THE WAY YOU

· ·

AND THE WAY YOU

·

· ·

YOU HELP ME
TO NOT TAKE
LIFE TOO

I'M REALLY GRATEFUL FOR THE WAY YOU MAKE ME

WHEN I'M FEELING DOWN IN THE DUMPS.

AND I'M ALWAYS
GRATEFUL FOR THE
LAUGHTER YOU
BRING ME... UNTIL

COMES SPILLING
OUT MY NOSE!

I WANTED TO
SAY THANK YOU
FOR ALMOST
EVERYTHING...

BUT THAT ONE TIME
YOU
....

....

....

SCARED ME TO DEATH!
I DEFINITELY DON'T
THANK YOU FOR THAT!

I'VE COME TO LEARN
THAT I MAY NOT HAVE

_____ ,

BUT I'LL ALWAYS HAVE

_____ .

FOR INSTANCE, I'LL ALWAYS HAVE YOU AND YOUR SELF!

_____

TRUE GRATITUDE IS NEVER TAKING

FOR GRANTED, ALWAYS APPRECIATING

-------- ,

AND MAKING SURE TO

IN ALL THE RAIN PUDDLES!

I FEEL *HONORED*
TO HAVE SUCH A

· ·

HUMAN BEING
FOR A ·.

WITHOUT YOU,

_____ ,

THE WORLD WOULD BE SO MUCH MORE

_____ .

THANKS TO YOU, I HAVEN'T BEEN ABLE TO STOP SINGING

TRULY...
AT 3 IN THE MORNING
OR EVEN AT ....
WHEN I SHOULD BE

.............................,
I REALLY CAN'T THANK
YOU ENOUGH FOR THIS
ABOMINABLE SONG
IN MY HEAD.

EVEN NOW,
MY MIND IS
BLOWN!

I STILL CAN'T BELIEVE HOW DANG GRACIOUS YOU WERE THAT ONE TIME THE

· ·

HIT THE FAN AND ALL

· ·

BROKE LOOSE!

THANKS FOR SAVING MY

_____

THAT TIME I

_____ !

YOU NEVER CEASE TO MAKE ME

WHEN EVERYTHING SEEMS BACKWARD AND INSIDE OUT.

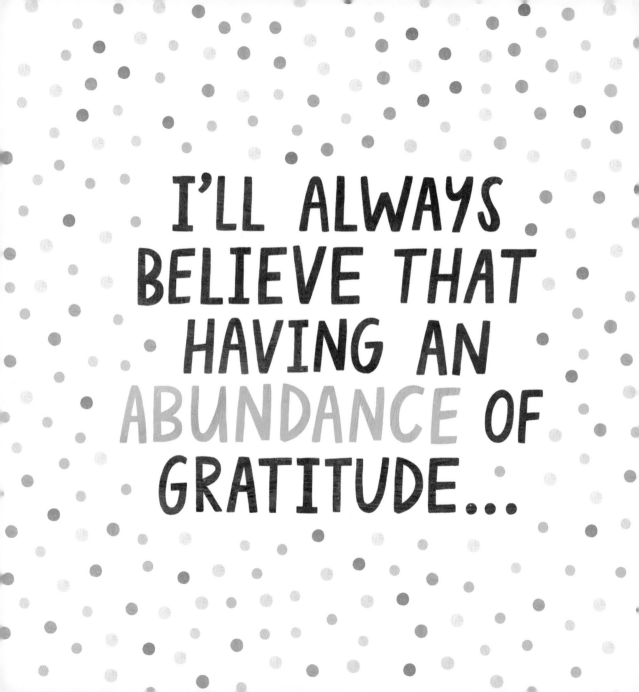

I'LL ALWAYS
BELIEVE THAT
HAVING AN
ABUNDANCE OF
GRATITUDE...

IS LIKE HAVING
AN ABUNDANCE OF

_____ .

YOU CAN NEVER
HAVE TOO MUCH!

I CAN'T HELP BUT LAUGH WHEN I REMEMBER THAT ONE TIME YOU

....

....

WHEN I WAS HAVING A BAD DAY!

I'M GRATEFUL FOR THE

YOU ALWAYS BRING TO MY LIFE.

YOU'VE HELPED ME TO LEARN THAT HAPPINESS ISN'T ALWAYS ABOUT GETTING

BUT ABOUT
LEARNING TO

--- •

I BELIEVE THERE
ARE SO MANY
DIFFERENT WAYS
TO SAY THANK YOU,
BUT HERE ARE
JUST A FEW:

YOU ARE SO DANG AWESOME AND COMPLETELY ....!
THANK YOU TIMES 10, TIMES ...., AND EVEN TIMES A MILLION!
YOU ARE A .... AND A .... AND A LIFE SAVER FOR SURE! YOU ARE THE MOST ....

PERSON I'VE EVER MET.

WHEN I FEEL LIKE I NEED TO

_____

_____

I'M SO GLAD BECAUSE I KNOW YOU'LL ALWAYS BE THERE.

YOU ARE BASICALLY THE

....

TO MY

....

IT MEANS THE
WORLD TO ME
THAT I CAN FEEL
EVERY EMOTION
AROUND YOU IF
I NEED TO...

I CRIED
WITH YOU WHEN

_____

_____ ,

AND I LAUGHED
WITH YOU WHEN

_____

_____ .

THANK YOU FOR BEING
THERE FOR ME.

YOU'RE MY ABSOLUTE
FAVORITE...............................
IN THE WHOLE WORLD!
THANK YOU FOR CHOOSING
ME AS YOUR...........................

SOMEHOW YOU
ALWAYS MANAGE
TO MAKE ME

_____

_____,

EVEN WHEN I DON'T
FEEL LIKE IT!

EVERY SINGLE DAY
I'M GRATEFUL FOR YOU.
FOR THE WAY YOU

------------------------------------,

THE FUNNY WAY YOU

------------------------------------,

AND THE COMPLETELY RIDICULOUS WAY YOU

--!

· ·

· ·

· ·

WAS PROBABLY THE BEST ADVICE YOU'VE EVER GIVEN TO ME.

I'VE FOLLOWED THIS ADVICE PROBABLY MORE THAN _____ TIMES!

WHEN LIFE THROWS A WRENCH INTO THINGS, YOU'RE THE PERFECT EXAMPLE OF BEING

_ _

AND _ _ _ _ _ _ _ _ _ _ _ _ _ _ _ _ .

THANK YOU. THANK YOU THANK YOU THANK YOU FOR ALL THOSE TIMES YOU'VE LISTENED TO ME

----------------------------------- .

I'LL JUST SAY IT —
SOMETIMES I CAN BE
A REAL PAIN IN THE

BUT EVEN SO, YOU ALWAYS SEEM TO

--- .

I'LL ALWAYS APPRECIATE THAT AMAZING WAY YOU KNOW JUST HOW TO

I NEVER QUITE
REALIZED I COULD

UNTIL YOU POINTED
THIS OUT TO ME!

ONE THING I'M REALLY GRATEFUL FOR ABOUT YOU...

IS THE WAY YOU NEVER SEEM TO

....................................:

EVEN WHEN

....

.... !

I'VE FOUND THAT BEING GRATEFUL FOR THE LITTLE THINGS HAS HELPED ME BE MORE GRATEFUL FOR THE BIG THINGS:

I'M GRATEFUL FOR_____;
IT'S THE ABSOLUTE BEST
CANDY BAR EVER MADE!

I'M SUPER THANKFUL FOR THE
SOUND OF_____.

_____ SMELLS AMAZING
ON A WARM SUMMER'S DAY.

A FIELD FULL OF_____
ALWAYS MAKES MY HEART FEEL
WARM AND FULL.

YOU'VE HELPED ME TO GROW AND EXPAND IN SO MANY WAYS.

I GREW A WHOLE

MILES WHEN YOU
TAUGHT ME TO

THANK YOU FOR INTRODUCING ME TO

ME TO

_____!

LIKE SERIOUSLY, HOW DID I EVER GET THROUGH LIFE HAVING NEVER TRIED

?

ON A SCALE FROM 1 TO 100, YOU'RE A

....

FOR SURE FOR THE AWESOME WAY YOU

...

....

AND MAYBE EVEN FOR THE COMPLETELY CRAZY WAY YOU

_____

_____ .

THANK YOU FOR
NEVER JUDGING
THE WEIRD WAY I

_____ ,

THE CRINGEWORTHY
WAY I

_____ ,

AND THE TOTALLY EMBARRASSING WAY I

_____ •

YOU'RE A TRUE

_____ •

THANK YOU FOR BEING THE FREAKISHLY REMARKABLE, CRAZILY INCREDIBLE, AND OUTRAGEOUSLY

· ·

HUMAN THAT YOU ARE!

YOU DESERVE TO BE PRAISED WITH ALL THE

_____

THE WORLD HAS TO OFFER.

MY FAVORITE PART OF

_____

WAS WHEN YOU TOOK ME TO

_____ .

IF I COULD LIKEN YOU TO A HISTORICAL FIGURE FOR HOW SUPER CARING YOU ARE, I'D CHOOSE

....

ONE OF MY FAVORITE HOLIDAY MEMORIES WITH YOU IS THAT TIME YOU

-------------------------------------- ...

I COULD NEVER
APPRECIATE YOU
MORE IN THAT
MOMENT BECAUSE
I FELT SO
_____
THAT DAY.

SOMETIMES
I FEEL LIKE
JUST SAYING
"THANK YOU"
ISN'T ENOUGH.

SO, IF I COULD, I'D GIVE
YOU THE WORLD'S BIGGEST
FULL OF A
_____
THOUSAND_____.
YOU DESERVE IT AND
SO MUCH MORE!

ANY DAY OF THE WEEK I'D
CHOOSE TO HAVE YOU AS MY
_____

RATHER THAN HAVING A
MILLION _____ ...

THANK YOU, FROM THE BOTTOM OF MY HEART, FOR THAT ONE TIME YOU

• •

IN FRONT OF EVERYBODY!

YOU MAY HAVE BEEN
MORTIFIED OR EVEN

- - - - - - - - - - - - - - - - - - - -

THAT IT HAPPENED,
BUT I'D VENTURE TO
SAY YOU MADE
EVERYONE'S DAY!
ESPECIALLY MINE!

OH MY STARS, YOU'RE SIMPLY AMAZING! I'VE ALWAYS APPRECIATED HOW HARD YOU'VE WORKED AT

THANK YOU SO MUCH FOR ALL OF YOUR

OVER THE YEARS.
I COULDN'T HAVE

WITHOUT YOU!

SOME MAY THINK IT A SIMPLE THING, BUT I'LL NEVER FORGET THAT TIME YOU TAUGHT ME

· ·

· ·

I THINK EVEN SMALL
ACTS OF KINDNESS
MEAN A WHOLE LOT
TO PEOPLE. I KNOW
IT MEANT A LOT TO

_____

WHEN YOU

_____

_____ .

SOME PEOPLE ARE JUST PLAIN OLD EVERYDAY PEOPLE. BUT YOU'RE NOT...

BECAUSE AT
HEART YOU'RE A

- - - - - - - - - - - - - - - - -

IN DISGUISE, A

- - - - - - - - - - - - - - - - -

FRIEND TO ALL, AND
BASICALLY THE BEST
EVER.

- - - - - - - - - - - -

SOME PEOPLE, LIKE YOU, ARE ALWAYS OUT THERE HELPING OTHERS. YOU

_ _

_ _

TO EVERYONE YOU SEE.

BASICALLY, YOU'RE A DIAMOND IN THE ROUGH, AND A .... IN THE ....

YOU'RE TRULY ONE OF A KIND.

I LOVE THE WAY YOU .... ,
THE SILLY WAY YOU .... ,
THE COMPLETELY EMBARRASSING,
BUT SUPERBLY AMAZING WAY YOU

.... ,

AND I ESPECIALLY LOVE THE WAY YOU

_____

_____.

THANK YOU SO MUCH FOR BEING YOU. I SURE CAN'T IMAGINE YOU BEING ANYONE ELSE.

GIBBS SMITH
TO ENRICH AND INSPIRE HUMANKIND

24 23 22 21 20   5 4 3 2 1

Written by Kenzie Lynne, © 2020 Gibbs Smith

Illustrated by Melanie Mikecz, © 2020 Melanie Mikecz

Published by
Gibbs Smith
P.O. Box 667
Layton, Utah 84041

1.800.835.4993 orders
www.gibbs-smith.com

Designed by Melanie Mikecz

Printed and bound in China
Gibbs Smith books are printed on either recycled, 100% post-consumer waste, FSC-certified papers or on paper produced from sustainable PEFC-certified forest/controlled wood source. Learn more at www.pefc.org.

ISBN: 978-1-4236-5425-4